KEY QUESTIONS
in AMERICAN HISTORY

WAS THE
HARLEM
RENAISSANCE
A RENAISSANCE?

ELIZABETH KRAJNIK

PowerKiDS
press.
New York

Published in 2019 by The Rosen Publishing Group, Inc.
29 East 21st Street, New York, NY 10010

First Edition

Editor: Elizabeth Krajnik
Book Design: Tanya Dellaccio

Photo Credits: Cover (Louis Armstrong) Bettmann/Getty Images; cover (Zora Neale Hurston) Fotosearch/Archive Photos/Getty Images; cover (band) Transcendental Graphics/Archive Photos/Getty Images; p. 5 Michael Ochs Archives/Getty Images; pp. 7, 11 (bottom) Courtesy of Library of Congress; p. 9 (top) Chicago History Museum/Archive Photos/Getty Images; p. 9 (bottom) Everett Historical/Shutterstock.com; pp. 11 (top), 13 (bottom) PhotoQuest/Archive Photos/Getty Images; p. 13 (top) https://commons.wikimedia.org/wiki/File:NellaLarsen1928.jpg; p. 15 (top) Library of Congress/Corbis Historical/Getty Images; p. 15 (bottom) Stock Montage/Archive Photos/Getty Images; p. 17 (top) Anthony Barboza/Archive Photos/Getty Images; p. 17 (bottom) Imagno/Hulton Archive/Getty Images; p. 19 John D. Kisch/Separate Cinema Archive/Moviepix/Getty Images; p. 21 Robert Abbott Sengstacke/Archive Photos/Getty Images; p. 23 (top) https://en.wikipedia.org/wiki/File:Augusta_Savage,_sculpting_-_NARA_-_559182.jpg https://en.wikipedia.org/wiki/File:Augusta_Savage,_sculpting_-_NARA_-_559182.jpg; p. 23 (bottom) The Washington Post/Getty Images; p. 25 https://commons.wikimedia.org/wiki/File:Sowing,_by_William_H._Johnson.jpg; p. 27 Michael Smith/Hulton Archive/Getty Images; p. 29 AFP Contributor/AFP/Getty Images.

Cataloging-in-Publication Data

Names: Krajnik, Elizabeth.
Title: Was the Harlem Renaissance a renaissance? / Elizabeth Krajnik.
Description: New York : PowerKids Press, 2019. | Series: Key questions in American history | Includes glossary and index.
Identifiers: LCCN ISBN 9781508167686 (pbk.) | ISBN 9781508167662 (library bound) | ISBN 9781508167693 (6 pack)
Subjects: LCSH: Harlem Renaissance–Juvenile literature. | African Americans–History–1877-1964–Juvenile literature. | African American arts–20th century–Juvenile literature. | African Americans–New York (State)–New York–Biography–Juvenile literature. | Harlem (New York, N.Y.)–Intellectual life–20th century–Juvenile literature. | New York (N.Y.)–Intellectual life–20th century–Juvenile literature.
Classification: LCC E185.6 K73 2019 | DDC 974.7'100496073–dc23

Manufactured in the United States of America

CPSIA Compliance Information: Batch #CS18PK: For Further Information contact Rosen Publishing, New York, New York at 1-800-237-9932

CONTENTS

A REBIRTH

Renaissance means "rebirth" in French. In the early 20th century, black **culture** underwent a period of rebirth known as the Harlem Renaissance. During this time, the United States— and the rest of the world—was going through many changes and new experiences. World War I and the Spanish **influenza** epidemic of 1918 led to many African Americans moving to northern states to start a new life free from poor treatment by southern white people.

The epicenter, or central point, of this renaissance was Harlem, New York. New publications arose and the movement spread. Traditionally African American types of music entered the mainstream. African American authors published many works of fiction, poetry, and drama. Many of these artists sought to produce works distinctive from those of white artists. Above all, African Americans celebrated their culture without regret or shame.

THE RENAISSANCE THEATRE (PICTURED HERE) PLAYED AN IMPORTANT ROLE IN THE DEVELOPMENT OF THE HARLEM RENAISSANCE. IT WAS DESIGNED, PAID FOR, BUILT, OWNED, AND RUN BY AFRICAN AMERICANS.

THE ROOTS OF THE RENAISSANCE

In 1865, the 13th Amendment abolished slavery, freeing millions of black people from captivity in the United States. Slavery had prevented many African Americans from receiving a formal education, limited their interaction with the outside world, and kept them from sharing many ideas. Even though the 14th Amendment in 1868 made the former slaves citizens of the United States, many white people still treated them like they were inferior.

During the era of Reconstruction from 1865 to 1877, however, many African Americans got a taste of greater freedoms. The 15th Amendment gave all male citizens the right to vote. Some African Americans served in the U.S. Congress and state legislatures. However, these freedoms were short lived. When Reconstruction ended, southern states passed laws to keep white people and black people separate. These laws are known as Jim Crow laws.

THIS IMAGE SHOWS THREE INFLUENTIAL BLACK MEN DURING RECONSTRUCTION. BLANCHE KELSO BRUCE (LEFT) AND HIRAM RHODES REVELS (RIGHT) WERE SENATORS AND FREDERICK DOUGLASS (CENTER) WAS A SPEAKER AND WRITER.

THE GREAT MIGRATION

Due to hostile treatment caused by Jim Crow laws and economic hardships in the South, many African Americans chose to move to the North and West. This movement during the 20th century is known as the Great Migration. Many black southerners moved to find jobs in northern factories, which experienced labor shortages due to the world wars and a decrease in **immigration**.

The larger cities to which African Americans moved experienced rapid growth. In just 10 years, the African American population in New York grew by 66 percent. These newcomers had to compete for housing, which often resulted in white people refusing to sell to African Americans. Housing rules created divided neighborhoods and caused relations between white people and African Americans to worsen.

THE KU KLUX KLAN (KKK) IS A WHITE SUPREMACIST HATE GROUP. THE KKK'S ORIGINAL GOAL WAS TO MAINTAIN WHITE SUPREMACY IN THE POST-CIVIL WAR SOUTH. A FORM OF THE GROUP IS STILL ACTIVE TODAY.

9

WHY HARLEM?

Harlem, a neighborhood in northern Manhattan in New York City, came to hold special meaning to African Americans during the early 20th century. Originally built as a neighborhood meant for white people, Harlem became an area where African Americans knew there was ample affordable housing. Many African Americans found a place to live there when they moved from the South to the North.

Even though many black people fled the South to escape **segregation** and **racism**, those practices were still present in the North. Harlem itself became one large segregated neighborhood, because many white people left as more African Americans moved there. It became a place where African Americans were able to share their personal experiences and create a movement to invest in their culture's traditions.

HARLEM HAD MANY POPULAR NIGHTCLUBS DURING THE RENAISSANCE PERIOD.

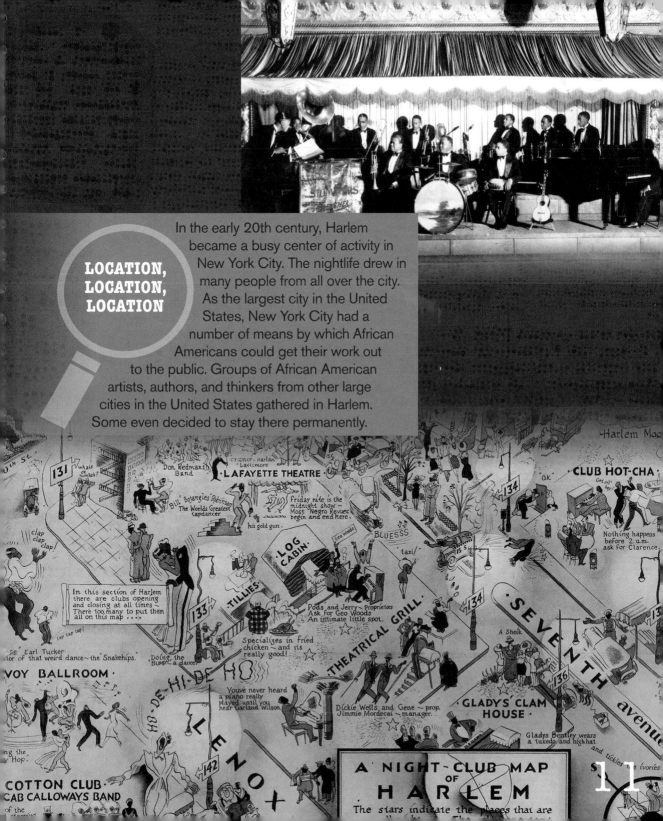

LOCATION, LOCATION, LOCATION

In the early 20th century, Harlem became a busy center of activity in New York City. The nightlife drew in many people from all over the city. As the largest city in the United States, New York City had a number of means by which African Americans could get their work out to the public. Groups of African American artists, authors, and thinkers from other large cities in the United States gathered in Harlem. Some even decided to stay there permanently.

A LITERARY MOVEMENT

Literature was one way African Americans could express themselves in a distinctly African American way—free from the **constraints** of what was considered white literature. This fact alone makes the Harlem Renaissance a rebirth, because African American literature was able to develop and grow.

Some of the greatest, most well-known novelists from the Harlem Renaissance include Langston Hughes, Zora Neale Hurston, James Weldon Johnson, W. E. B. Du Bois, and Jessie Redmon Fauset. Their novels cover many topics, but many of the novels written during the Harlem Renaissance focus on the African American experience. These novels were often seen as very modern for that time and approached topics not previously discussed. Walter White's *The Fire in the Flint* explores racism and how white **oppression** often prevented African Americans from becoming successful.

HISTORIC MOMENTS

Zora Neale Hurston's novel *Their Eyes Were Watching God* was turned into a feature film starring Halle Berry in 2005.

12

NELLA LARSEN WAS ANOTHER WELL-KNOWN AND RESPECTED FEMALE AFRICAN AMERICAN AUTHOR. SHE WROTE THE NOVELS *QUICKSAND* (1928) AND *PASSING* (1929).

NOT JUST NOVELS

Many novelists from this time also created other literary works, such as poems and short stories. Zora Neale Hurston, for example, also wrote short stories such as *The Gilded Six-Bits* and created collections of African American folk tales such as *Every Tongue Got to Confess*. Hurston also worked with Langston Hughes to write *Mule Bone*, a play. This work wasn't performed until 60 years after it was written.

NELLA LARSEN

ZORA NEALE HURSTON

African American poetry also experienced a rebirth during the Harlem Renaissance. Some poets, such as Countee Cullen, believed that traditionally white forms of poetry were a part of his **heritage** just as much as they were a part of white Americans' heritage. However, Langston Hughes believed that African American poetry should shy away from white poetic forms and language. He said black poets should create poetry that was distinctly African American.

Hughes's opinion fed into larger discussions about racism at the time. Some people believed that black people from the South were in some ways free from white influence—more so than the African Americans who had spent most of their lives surrounded by white people and their art forms. Some poets chose to model their work after black southern preachers' sermons. Other poets used folk songs and jazz music as inspiration.

FOUNDED IN 1910, THE *CRISIS: A RECORD OF THE DARKER RACES* WAS ONE WAY WRITERS OF THE HARLEM RENAISSANCE COULD GET THEIR WORK SEEN BY THE MASSES. JESSIE REDMON FAUSET'S TIME AS LITERARY EDITOR, FROM 1919 TO 1926, WERE SOME OF THE MOST PROSPEROUS YEARS FOR THE MAGAZINE.

JESSIE
REDMON
FAUSET

THE CRISIS

A RECORD OF THE DARKER RACES

Volume One	NOVEMBER, 1910	Number One

Edited by W. E. BURGHARDT DU BOIS, with the co-operation of Oswald Garrison Villard, J. Max Barber, Charles Edward Russell, Kelly Miller, W. S. Braithwaite and M. D. Maclean.

CONTENTS

PUBLISHED MONTHLY BY THE

National Association for the Advancement of Colored People

AT TWENTY VESEY STREET   NEW YORK CITY

ONE DOLLAR A YEAR   TEN CENTS A COPY

15

MAKING MUSIC

During the Harlem Renaissance, jazz and blues music began to enter the American mainstream. A number of previously unknown blues musicians and singers, such as Bessie Smith, Alberta Hunter, and Ma Rainey, became famous at an unexpected rate. This was due, in part, to "race records," or music recordings made by and for African Americans. Over time, more white people started to look for and buy the records.

The blues often told the stories of working-class African Americans and their struggles. From the blues came jazz, another musical style. During the 1920s, jazz grew to feature new instruments, a new performance style, and larger bands. One notable feature of jazz music is improvisation, or changing or making up parts of the music as you go.

HISTORIC MOMENTS

Many dance moves developed alongside jazz music. The Charleston and tap dance became internationally popular during the Harlem Renaissance.

FROM THE BLUES TO RAP

The blues have given rise to many other types of music. From blues came jazz. Blues also influenced the development of soul music and rhythm and blues. The blues even influenced classical musicians, who used some of the style in their own compositions, such as Gershwin's "Rhapsody in Blue." Rock and roll musicians, such as Elvis Presley, drew upon the blues and jazz to create their music. Hip-hop and rap also have roots in the blues tradition. Without the blues, the music we know and love today might not exist.

DIZZY GILLESPIE WAS A JAZZ TRUMPETER, COMPOSER, AND BANDLEADER. IN THE MID-1940s, HE AND COLEMAN HAWKINS FOUNDED THE BEBOP MOVEMENT. IN THE LATE 1940s, GILLESPIE FORMED HIS OWN JAZZ GROUP, WHICH PERFORMED BEBOP AND AFRO-CUBAN JAZZ.

17

A number of extremely talented jazz musicians became popular during the Harlem Renaissance. Duke Ellington was perhaps the greatest jazz composer and bandleader. He got his start in Washington, D.C., and moved to New York City in 1923. In New York, he performed in Broadway nightclubs. In the early 1940s, Ellington created a musical composition (*Black, Brown and Beige*) that explored how jazz could be composed within a classical-music framework. African American musicians such as Ellington set the tone for much American music for many years to come.

The popularity of jazz music inspired other African Americans to draw upon their heritage and create their own art. Musicals and other shows produced by black people and featuring black performers spread and gained attention.

BLACK AND TAN IS A MUSICAL SHORT FILM IN WHICH DUKE ELLINGTON AND HIS GROUP PERFORM AS A JAZZ BAND. THE FILM TAKES PLACE IN NEW YORK CITY DURING THE HARLEM RENAISSANCE.

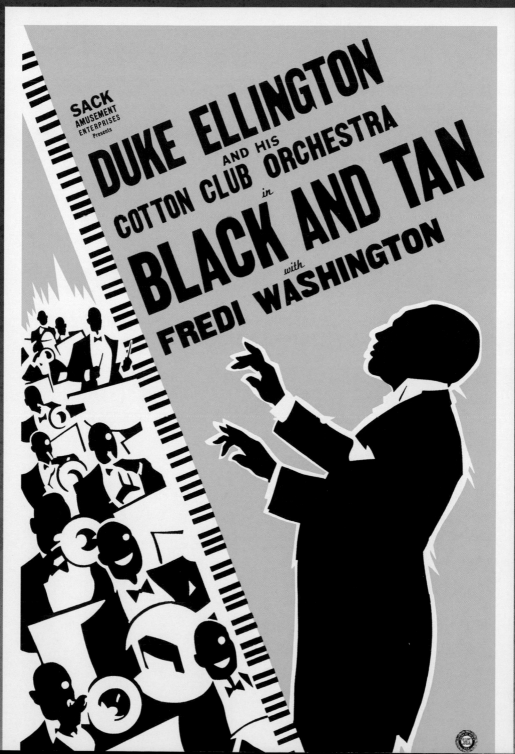

19

CREATIVE SELF-EXPRESSION

Visual artists during the Harlem Renaissance also worked to create pieces that dealt with African American subjects and were less influenced by white art. Up until this time, many African American artists worked within the frameworks set forth by white artists. Creative self-expression was a way for African American artists to make their mark.

After the Great Depression, many artists returned to the United States from abroad. New York City became a focus for artists and their craft. Art schools, galleries, and museums cropped up, making art more accessible to a new generation of African Americans. In 1937, the Harlem Community Art Center opened, giving young people more opportunities to explore their own creative self-expression.

AARON DOUGLAS, ONE OF THE MOST FAMOUS ARTISTS OF THE HARLEM RENAISSANCE, WAS INFLUENCED BY A NUMBER OF DIFFERENT ART STYLES, INCLUDING ANCIENT EGYPTIAN ART. DOUGLAS PAINTED **MURALS** AND CREATED ILLUSTRATIONS AND COVER DESIGNS FOR MANY BLACK PUBLICATIONS DURING THE HARLEM RENAISSANCE.

BLACK FEMALE ARTISTS

The Harlem Renaissance produced a number of notable female artists. Augusta Savage was a sculptor who got her start modeling clay figures in her home state of Florida when she was very young. In 1921, Savage moved to New York to study art at Cooper Union for the Advancement of Science and Art, where she impressed her instructors. She studied in Paris from 1929 to 1931 and then returned to New York to teach art. She founded the Savage Studio of Arts and Crafts in Harlem in 1932.

Lois Mailou Jones was a painter from Boston, Massachusetts. She painted in several different styles, including traditional African styles. She also designed masks, and a number of her works feature them. From 1937 to 1938, Jones studied painting at the Académie Julian in Paris, where she painted many landscapes and street scenes.

AUGUSTA SAVAGE CREATED A SCULPTURE IN NEW YORK CITY AS AN ART SERVICE PROJECT. THE PAINTING (BELOW) BEHIND LOIS MAILOU JONES IS TITLED *MOB VICTIM* AND SHOWS HER STYLE OF PAINTING MASKS.

The 19th Amendment

During the early years of the Harlem Renaissance, women won the right to vote in elections in the United States. On August 18, 1920, the required number of states finally ratified the 19th Amendment to the U.S. Constitution. This amendment says no citizen can be denied the right to vote based on sex. However, women still didn't have the same opportunities as men. Even while African Americans explored new ways to express themselves, African American women had to work even harder to be noticed as artists.

23

PRIMITIVISM

The Harlem Renaissance was a time of changing philosophies. One such trend was primitivism. Cultural primitivism is the idea that people should return to a simpler way of life. Primitivism can also refer to placing importance on what is natural or basically human.

The influence of primitivism can be seen throughout the art of the Harlem Renaissance in the artists' return to African folk styles. Some authors, such as Zora Neale Hurston and Langston Hughes, chose to write in dialects that reflected their natural voices rather than writing in the English most white people wrote and spoke. Some artists rejected the ideas of primitivism because they were concerned about **stereotypes**. Still, the trend did bring new attention to these art forms.

SOME OF THE WORK BY ARTIST WILLIAM H. JOHNSON USES THE TRENDS OF PRIMITIVISM. JOHNSON USED FEW COLORS AND A FLAT STYLE IN SOME OF HIS WORKS, SUCH AS *SOWING*, SHOWN HERE.

ORGANIZATIONS
FUEL THE MOVEMENT

Organizations we still recognize today played an important role in fueling the Harlem Renaissance. They helped bring attention to the works of many African American authors, composers, singers, and artists.

The National Association for the Advancement of Colored People (NAACP) was one of the most important organizations associated with the Harlem Renaissance. The NAACP gave a voice to many black writers. It also fought for the passage of a law prohibiting **lynching**. This bill, known as the Dyer Bill, aimed to change how white and black people interacted. However, the bill was never passed.

The National Urban League (NUL) worked toward helping African Americans participate fully in American life. In the early 20th century, the NUL, headquartered in New York City, helped people moving to the city find jobs and housing.

TODAY, THE NAACP CONTINUES TO FIGHT FOR EQUALITY FOR ALL PEOPLE.

Organizational Publications

Many of the organizations that helped fuel the Harlem Renaissance spread the word through magazines. The NAACP published The *Crisis* and the NUL published *Opportunity*. These publications gave young authors a chance to share their ideas and gain a following. The editors of these magazines discovered many young black writers, who gained the attention of both black and white readers. Without these publications, we might have never heard of Langston Hughes or Zora Neale Hurston.

27

WAS IT A RENAISSANCE?

The Harlem Renaissance brought new artists, authors, and musicians to the spotlight. But was the Harlem Renaissance truly a rebirth? If the forms of art that became popular during this time were all new, that would mean it was a birth, not a rebirth. However, even though jazz music was a new creation at the time, it was still a rebirth of African American creative expression through music and it was rooted in older traditions. This also applies to other forms of creative expression popular during the Harlem Renaissance.

The Harlem Renaissance was a rebirth of African cultural traditions. Without this rebirth, many of the African American creators of the past 100 years, such as authors Toni Morrison, Octavia Butler, Ta-Nehisi Coates, and Sharon Draper; musicians Ray Charles, Jimi Hendrix, Beyoncé, and John Legend; and many other artists might not have had the chance to produce the works we know and love today.

MARTIN LUTHER KING JR.

THE HARLEM RENAISSANCE BROUGHT AFRICAN AMERICAN CONCERNS AND VIEWS INTO THE PUBLIC EYE. IT CREATED A FOUNDATION THAT WOULD LATER GIVE RISE TO THE CIVIL RIGHTS MOVEMENT AND ACTIVISTS SUCH AS MARTIN LUTHER KING JR.

29

TIMELINE

FEBRUARY 12, 1909

W. E. B. Du Bois and several others found the NAACP.

1910

The NAACP starts The *Crisis* with Du Bois as the founding editor. Its first issue is published in November.

1916

Black families begin to move to the North. This event is known as The Great Migration.

NOVEMBER 11, 1918

World War I ends.

1918–1919

The Spanish influenza epidemic kills as many as 50 million people worldwide.

AUGUST 18, 1920

The United States ratifies the 19th Amendment to the U.S. Constitution.

1921

Augusta Savage moves to New York City.

1923

Duke Ellington moves to New York City.

1924

Walter White's novel *The Fire in the Flint* is published.

1932

Savage founds the Savage Studio of Arts and Crafts in Harlem.

SEPTEMBER 18, 1937

Zora Neale Hurston's novel *Their Eyes Were Watching God* is published.

JANUARY 23, 1943

Duke Ellington and his musicians perform *Black, Brown and Beige* at Carnegie Hall.

GLOSSARY

constraint: Something that limits or holds back someone or something.

culture: The beliefs and ways of life of a certain group of people.

heritage: The traditions and beliefs that are part of the history of a group or nation.

immigration: The act of coming to a country to settle there.

influenza: A common illness that is caused by a virus and that causes fever, weakness, severe aches and pains, and breathing problems.

lynch: To kill someone, usually by hanging, through mob action and without legal permission.

mural: A usually large painting that is done directly on the surface of a wall.

oppression: The state of being treated in a cruel or unjust way.

racism: The belief that one group or race of people is better than another group or race.

segregation: The separation of people based on race, class, or ethnicity.

stereotype: An often unfair, untrue belief that people may have about people or things of a certain kind.

supremacist: A person who believes that one group of people is better than all other groups and should have control over them.

INDEX

WEBSITES

Due to the changing nature of Internet links, PowerKids Press has developed an online
list of websites related to the subject of this book. This site is updated regularly. Please
use this link to access the list: www.powerkidslinks.com/kqah/harrren